BLAC[illegible] No. 82

Ed[illegible]agg

HERALDRY

by

JOHN BROOKE-LITTLE

MVO, MA, FSA, Richmond Herald

Illustrated by Peter Spurrier

BASIL BLACKWELL OXFORD

First Published 1975

0 631 13190 6

Author's Note

Many of the special words in this book are not easy to pronounce. There is a list of these on page 61, with some help for you in saying them. When you come across a strange word in the book, see if it is in the list.

CONTENTS

Perhaps you have seen shields painted with birds, animals, castles and all sorts of other shapes. You may have seen them in stained glass windows or on tombs in churches. They may be outside banks, shops or offices in your local town. Or you may have seen some in books and magazines.

You can see some of them opposite, and you can probably draw others which you know. Have you ever wondered what they are, where they came from and what they mean?

The study of the pictures on these shields is called heraldry, and in fact some of them are very old, with long and interesting histories. All the parts of the shields mean something, and those parts sometimes have strange names.

In this book you will read about how heraldry started, and about the names and

shapes of some of the things which you see on these shields. You may even, by the end, be able to design a shield for yourself.

THE FIRST COATS OF ARMS

Just over 900 years ago England was conquered by a Norman Duke called William. He came over the sea from Normandy, which is in the north of France, with a large army and won the Battle of Hastings against King Harold in the year 1066. Harold was killed and William, whom we call William the Conqueror, was crowned King of England.

As king he owned all the land of England but he divided it up and gave it to his Norman friends. In return they had to come to help the king when he needed them, bringing their own men to fight. So in time of war many soldiers came together under their leaders, knights and lords, to make one big army.

A Norman Knight

The picture on page 7 shows a Norman knight in full armour. Look carefully at it. The knight's body is covered with mail, which is like a garment knitted not with wool but with steel. Over it he wears a loose coat called the coat-armour, which helped to protect him from sword-blows. On his head is a helmet with a piece of metal coming down over his nose. This guarded his nose, but it also made it hard to be sure who he was, because his face could not be seen properly.

You can imagine how difficult it was for the king to tell who the leaders were, for the leaders to know each other, and for the soldiers to know their own lord!

How would you mark the knights so that all would know who was who? Would you write their names on their coat-armour? That would not do because few people–even important people–could read in those days.

In fact what the knights did was to paint a bold and bright shape, or design, on their shields, and also on their coat-armour, flags, and horse-covering. They did this so that everyone could tell who they were, even from a long way away. Because these designs were painted on their coat-armour they came to be called "coats of arms", or just "arms". Look at the coloured picture of a knight opposite page 15. Notice the design which he has chosen.

What sort of things do you think the knights and lords picked for their coats of arms? The answer is all sorts of things, but they were usually symbols rather than pictures. A symbol is a simple shape which stands for something else, just as the cross is the symbol of Jesus Christ and Christianity, because Jesus died on a cross.

A lion or an eagle stand for courage because they are both bold, fierce creatures.

A lily is the symbol of Mary the mother of Jesus, and a book is a symbol of learning. What other symbols can you think of?

Here are some of the symbols used by knights on their coats of arms in early days.

You know that your surname is the same as your father's, and it is your family name. Family names are passed on to children, and coats of arms are passed down in the same way. But each person has to have a coat of arms which is different from everyone else's, so sons place their own special mark on their family shield. An eldest son adds a label (like a comb with three teeth) whilst his father is alive. A second son adds a crescent, a third son a star, a fourth a little bird called a martlet, and so on. In this way you can tell to which family a man belongs by the design of his shield, and his place in that family by the little symbol, usually put at the top.

Here is the coat of arms of a fourth son. Can you see the martlet?

THE FIRST HERALDS

There had to be rules about coats of arms. For example, someone had to make sure that two people didn't use the same design. Also the designs had to be simple and easy to understand. Coats of arms needed to be designed by people who were artistic and who understood symbols.

Records had to be kept showing who had which coat of arms. Otherwise the knights, who were proud of their arms, might quarrel. Coats of arms were used only by the leaders, so they thought of them as something which showed how important they were. They felt that a coat of arms was a great honour.

The men who looked after the design and use of coats of arms were called heralds.

These men had a number of duties at the courts of the king and his great nobles. Both in peace and in war they acted as messengers. They helped to bring together the king's army in wartime, and they made lists of the leaders who were present. At other times they arranged tournaments, and acted as referees.

Tournaments were great mock battles when knights could show off their skill and courage, and here, as in real battles, they were recognised by their coats of arms. You can see a coloured picture of a tournament facing page 30.

Look for the coats of arms of the knights.

Which of the men do you think are the heralds?

Because of their work in arranging tournaments, as well as in gathering armies

One of the first uses of coats of arms

together, you can tell that the heralds needed to know all about the coats of arms of the knights. Indeed, it may be that the idea of having coats of arms in the first place was something to do with the heralds. We do know for certain that the heralds had a lot to do with coats of arms from very early times, and that they soon began to make rules about what could or could not be shown on a shield.

It is because of the heralds' great interest in coats of arms that the study of arms is called heraldry.

HERALDRY TODAY

You may be surprised to know that there are still heralds today. For many hundreds of years the senior heralds, called "kings of arms", have granted coats of arms to people, and have kept records of what they have done. They do not act as messengers or gather armies together now, and there are no tournaments. But today the Queen's heralds still help to arrange and take part in great ceremonies of state.

You can recognise a herald at these ceremonies by his ancient and splendid uniform which is called a tabard. As you can see in the picture opposite, this is a loose coat which has a coat of arms on the front, the back, and on either sleeve. This is the Queen's coat of arms.

There are nine royal heralds now, and three of these are called kings of arms. Then there are four junior heralds called *pursuivants*. The heralds have their offices and keep their records in a building in London called the College of Arms. Here they give advice on heraldry, ceremonies, and the coats of arms of families over the years.

You can see the College opposite.

The kings of arms, heralds and pursuivants have old and often curious titles. The senior English king of arms is called Garter King of Arms, and the two other kings of arms are Clarenceux King of Arms, and Norroy and Ulster King of Arms. The writer of this book is called Richmond Herald, and there are also Chester, Somerset, Windsor, Lancaster and York Heralds. The pursuivants are Portcullis, Bluemantle, Rouge Dragon and Rouge Croix.

These strange and beautiful names go back to the early days of history and are part of the history of our country.

COATS OF ARMS IN USE

You remember that coats of arms were first used to make it easy to know who the knights were in battles or tournaments. Battles are no longer fought by knights on horseback, and tournaments have not been held for well over 300 years, so why do you think coats of arms are still used?

Do you remember that a coat of arms was regarded as an honour, because arms were only given to knights and noblemen? People were proud of their coats of arms, and so they still held on to them even after they did not need them for war or tournaments. They easily found other uses for them, and one of these uses was on seals.

Today, as you probably know, your signature is important. Signing your name to something means that you agree to whatever you have signed. Your signature shows that you have made a promise. But in the old days, when many people could not read or write, a seal was often used instead of a signature.

To make a seal, a piece of metal with a design on it was pressed on to hot wax, leaving a clear shape in the wax. The best shape to have on your seal was a picture of your coat of arms. This would make it clear to everyone, whether they could read or not, exactly whose seal it was.

Here is an example of a seal.

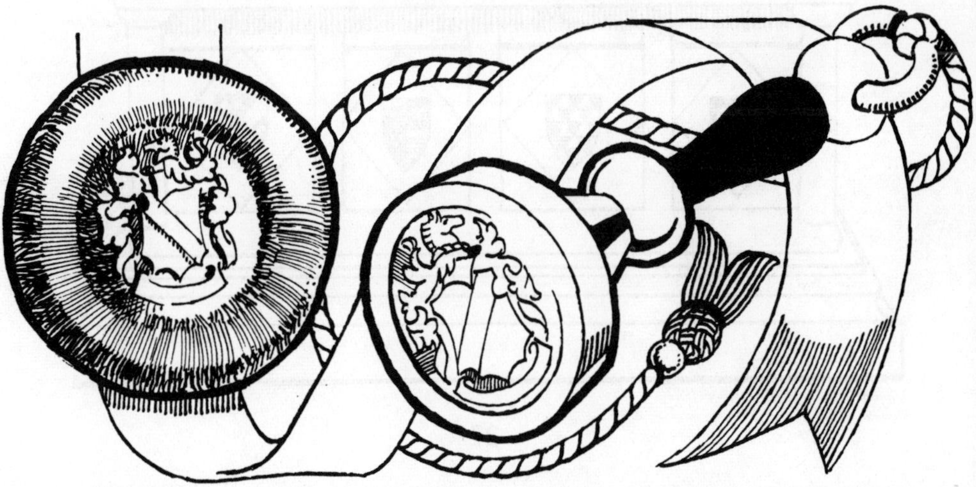

Nowadays seals are still used for some purposes. Try to find out about these.

Arms were also used on tombs where people were buried. An effigy (or model) of the dead person wearing full armour decorated with his arms was put on his tomb. Often the sides of the tomb were decorated with the coats of arms of his relations. Here is a tomb of this kind.

Perhaps you write your name inside your books, or have your initials transferred on to your bicycle. In the time of the Normans, as you have read, few people could write and there were no transfers. But there were coats of arms, so if a person wanted to show that he owned a certain thing, such as a plate or a mug, he often marked it with a picture of his arms. This showed that it was his, but it also made it look interesting and perhaps beautiful.

Look at these examples.

The pictures above show some ways in which coats of arms have been used to decorate things or to show ownership. Can you think of other ways in which you might have used a coat of arms if you had been a Norman knight? Can you think of ways in which you might use a coat of arms today?

THE QUEEN'S ARMS

The first English king to have a proper coat of arms on his seal was Richard I, who died in 1199. He used three golden lions on a red shield. This coat of arms is still part of the Queen's arms today, together with the lion of Scotland and the harp of Ireland. Look at this below.

You can also see the Queen's arms in colour next to page 54, and you will notice that there is much more than just a shield. There is a belt round the shield on which you can see the words "Honi soit qui mal y pense". A lion and a unicorn hold the shield on either side. Above is a helmet on which stands a lion. On the grassy mount on which the lion and unicorn stand is a scroll with the words "Dieu et mon droit".

You may think that all this is a muddle, but if we look at the separate parts we shall see that each part is there for some reason. So let us look at the Queen's arms to help to understand other coats of arms, too.

The *shield* you know about. On it are the arms of the Queen which are those of England, Scotland and Ireland. The arms of England are repeated to fill up the shield.

The lion standing on the crown on top of the *helmet* is called a *crest*. Knights began to use crests on the helmets they wore about a hundred years after they started using coats of arms.

The pictures show some crests which were used in the fourteenth century, in the time of King Edward III.

It was not long before crests, like arms, were handed down from father to son. Just as arms were shown on seals or used for decoration, so were crests. And because the crest was fixed to the helmet, it seemed silly not to show it without the helmet in seals or pictures. So the helmet was shown too.

Fastened to the real helmet worn by knights there was also a short cloak called a *lambrequin* or *mantling*. This was shown with coats of arms as well. By making the mantlings large and showy, artists were able to produce very pleasant designs of shields and crests. Look for this on the Queen's arms.

We do not know what the real mantling was for. Perhaps it helped to stop a sword from hitting the neck. The sword would strike the mantling which would deaden the blow. Also it may have helped to keep the sun from the back of the helm.

Now look again at the Queen's arms. Beneath the crest is a *crown*, showing that the person is a king or queen. Most crests have something like this where they are fixed to the helmet. Usually it is a sort of *wreath*, like two twisted scarves. Sometimes the crest comes out from a *coronet* (a small crown), while other crests rest on noblemen's caps called *chapeaux* or *caps of estate*. The pictures show various ways in which the join between the crest and the helmet is hidden.

a wreath

a coronet

a chapeau

a mural crown

On one side of the Queen's shield is a lion, and on the other a unicorn. Because these beasts are shown as if they are holding the shield between them they are called *supporters*. Supporters were first used towards the end of the fifteenth century. King Henry VII's shield was sometimes supported by a dragon and a greyhound, and sometimes by a lion and a dragon.

Supporters were added to the shields of

Knights at a tournament

great noblemen by artists and engravers. The beasts they used usually had something to do with the heraldry of the family, and because of this the heralds made rules about them. One rule is that they are given only to noblemen and very important knights. Another is that only the head of a family may use the supporters with his arms.

The mound of grass on which the Queen's supporters stand is called the *compartment*. It is not part of the coat of arms and can be left out, but it is usual to give the supporters something to stand on.

Below the compartment is a *scroll* which contains a motto. A motto is a family slogan or war-cry. The royal motto is French and means "My God and my right". Most mottoes are in Latin or French, but they can be found in many other languages. The heralds do not control mottoes but let people use what they please. So don't be surprised if you find different families using the same motto.

The belt round the Queen's shield represents a garter, and shows that the Queen is the head of the Order of the Garter.

For hundreds of years there have been various "orders" with interesting names, to which knights have belonged. There are, for example, the Knights of the Bath, the Knights of St. Michael and St. George, and the Knights of the British Empire. Each order has a motto, and the knights belonging to that order may place the motto round their shields.

The motto of the Order of the Garter, on the Queen's shield, is French and means "Evil be to him who evil thinks"–or "You should not think evil thoughts".

A complete coat of arms is called an achievement of arms, and the Queen's arms should have helped to show you what a full achievement looks like. Do you remember the names of the different parts of the achievement?

First of all there is the simple coat of arms, on a shield. Almost all arms also have a crest, which is shown above the shield, fixed to the helm which has a mantling at the back of it. Sometimes the helmet and the mantling are left out and the crest sits on top of the shield or floats over it. This is not wrong but it is rather ugly. It seems silly to leave out the helmet to which the real crest was once fixed.

Beneath the shield many families have a scroll with a motto. Nobles and important knights also have supporters on either side of their shields, perhaps standing on a mound called a compartment. Knights show the mottoes of their orders round their shields.

MAKING A COAT OF ARMS

Have you ever noticed that schools, towns, banks and other places often use coats of arms nowadays? Just look around you in any town. You will probably see the arms of the town itself on lamp-posts, signs and buildings, as well as the arms of banks hanging outside them, and the arms of some companies shown on their offices.

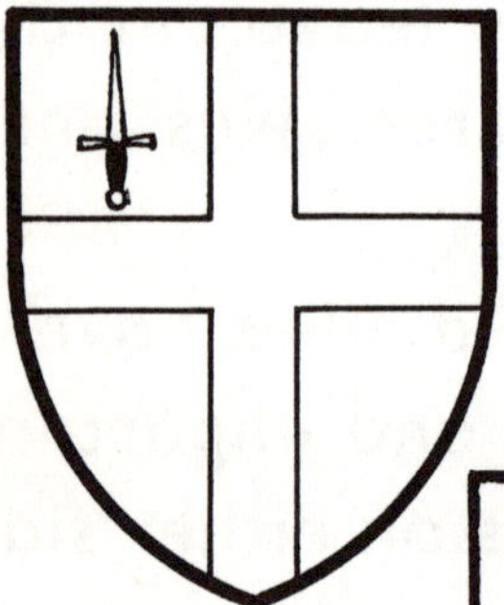

City of London

University of Cambridge

Worshipful Company of Scriveners

Have you a shield on the pocket of your blazer? Many schools have a coat of arms. Since the early days of heraldry towns, schools, etc., just as much as people, have wanted to use a symbol. They like to mark their property, fly a flag, or show who they are by using a colourful symbol. What could be better than using a coat of arms?

A coat of arms is an honourable symbol for anyone. It makes a pleasant picture, and records of it are kept by the heralds. So after a time the Kings of Arms began to give coats of arms to towns, universities, schools, and all sorts of bodies and people who seemed to deserve them.

Let us look now at how such coats of arms are made up.

If you were a herald, how would you start to design a coat of arms? What colours and symbols would you use? You can in fact use almost anything!

Suppose, for example, you were designing a coat of arms for a famous general. You might make the background of the shield red and put two swords on it. The red might stand for the red coat of a soldier and the two swords for fighting.

But before we look more closely at the colours and objects to use on coats of arms, there are six more words for you to learn:

The *field* of a shield means the surface or background of the shield.

Charge means any shape or object used on the field.

Chief means the top of the shield.

Base means the bottom of the shield.

Dexter means the right-hand side of the shield.

Sinister means the left-hand side of the shield.

There is one catch about *dexter* and *sinister*, however. They do not mean the right and left as you look at the shield, but the opposite! A herald always thinks of a shield as if he is behind it and carrying it (as a knight did). So the right–dexter–is on your left as you look at it, and the left–sinister–is on your right as you look at it, like this:

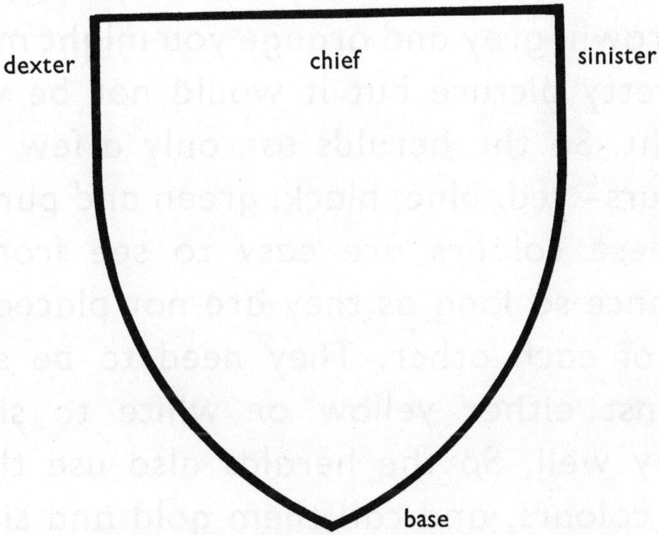

Animals on shields usually face and move to the dexter of the shield, as you saw on the Queen's shield–that is, your left as you look at it.

Now let us think about what makes up a coat of arms.

Colours, metals and furs

The first thing to remember is that a coat of arms must be easy to see from a distance. It must show up well. If you use colours such as brown, grey and orange you might make a pretty picture but it would not be very bright. So the heralds use only a few rich colours– red, blue, black, green and purple.

These colours are easy to see from a distance so long as they are not placed on top of each other. They need to be seen against either yellow or white to show really well. So the heralds also use these two colours, and call them gold and silver (metals).

Thus the heralds' paint box has five colours and two metals, and the rule is that you never place a colour on top of another colour, nor a metal on a metal. For example, if you want to put a red lion on a shield, then the shield must be either gold or silver (yellow or white).

The colours and metals are not called by their English names, but by words taken from other languages known to the early heralds. This is true of many of the words in heraldry. Here are the correct names of the colours and metals:

Red is *gules.*

Blue is *azure.*

Black is *sable.*

Green is *vert.*

Purple is *purpure.*

Gold is *or.*

Silver is *argent.*

Most of these words come from French, for that was the language spoken by most educated people when heraldry first started.

As well as the colours and metals the

heralds also use two furs, called *ermine* and *vair*. Ermine is a white fur spattered with black tails. It was used to trim the gowns of rich noblemen and is still used in royal and noble robes. Vair is made of little squirrel skins coloured blue and white. It was a less valuable fur used in the middle ages. The furs are useful to show on shields because they may be put on or beneath either a colour or a metal.

"Ordinaries"

The simplest *charges*—objects on shields—are just shapes rather than real things. These are called *ordinaries*, and here are some. Notice their strange names.

fess pale chief

chevron

cross

saltire

pile

bend

pall

Other, less important shapes are called *sub-ordinaries*, and you can see some of these here.

inescutcheon

bordure

fret

orle

mascle

flaunches

Animals and Monsters

Perhaps the next most usual charges are living creatures. Some are those which you might see in a zoo, except that they are usually shown in special positions, and not as you might see them in their cages. Also there are some creatures that you would not find in any zoo. These are monsters such as dragons, unicorns, griffins and mermaids. You can see pictures of some of these on page 47.

The lion is by far the commonest beast in coats of arms, but boars, rams, horses, bulls, bears, stags and many smaller creatures are found. You see them in many different positions, and all these positions have special names. For example, if the head of a beast does not face the right (dexter), but is looking straight out at us it is *guardant*. If it is looking over its shoulder it is *reguardant*. The Queen's lions are *passant guardant* because they are walking along *(passant)* as well as looking out at us. Look at the pictures to show the names given to some of these positions of heraldic creatures.

sejant

courant

couchant guardant

boar passant

bull rampant

goat salient

lion statant guardant

Birds

Among the birds the eagle is shown most often, usually as you see it here.

Another favourite bird is the martlet, which looks like the swift, swallow or martin. Those three birds always seem to have no legs, so martlets appear without legs in heraldry. Falcons, because they are hunting birds, are often found in coats of arms, and pelicans, cranes, peacocks, owls and choughs are not uncommon.

peacock in his pride

falcon rising

owl

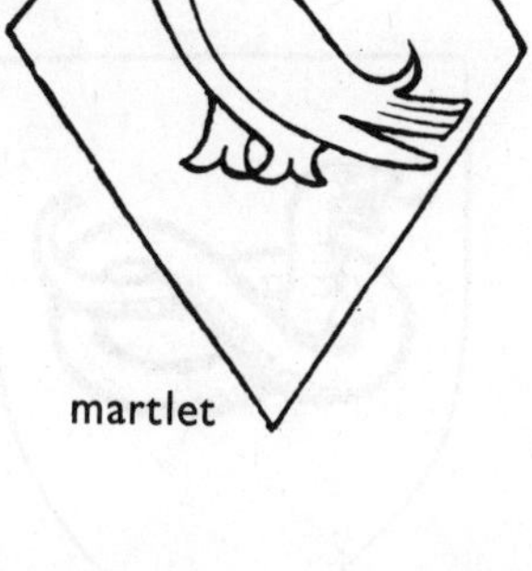

martlet

chough

Other creatures

An old English name for the pike—a fresh-water fish—was a *lucy*, and this is its name in heraldry. Lucies and dolphins are the favourite heraldic fish, but you will find anything from a salmon to a crab in coats of arms.

lucy

dolphin naiant (swimming)

The serpent *nowed* (which means tied in a knot) is the commonest reptile, and the bee *volant* (which means flying upwards) is the most usual insect.

bee volant

serpent nowed

Then there are the monsters which you read about earlier. The pictures show what some of them look like.

unicorn rampant

griffin statant

dragon passant

yale passant

sea lion

sea horse

If you are thinking that the sea lion and the sea horse do not look like those you may have seen in a zoo, you are quite right. Heralds make sea monsters by putting fish's tails and fins on to animals or even other monsters. Perhaps you can invent one. What about a sea-pig or a sea-cow?

Human beings are sometimes found in arms, but more likely as crests or supporters. Parts of humans and also parts of other creatures are very common. Heads, hands, legs and paws are very popular. It is also usual to cut a creature in two and just show the top half. When this is done it is said to be *demi*, which means half.

Growing things

Flowers, trees, leaves and fruit are much used. Some of these, such as the rose, fluer-de-lys (lily), trefoil, quatrefoil and cinquefoil do not always look exactly like the real ones. But pears, pineapples, acorns, leaves and various trees and flowers are drawn as in nature.

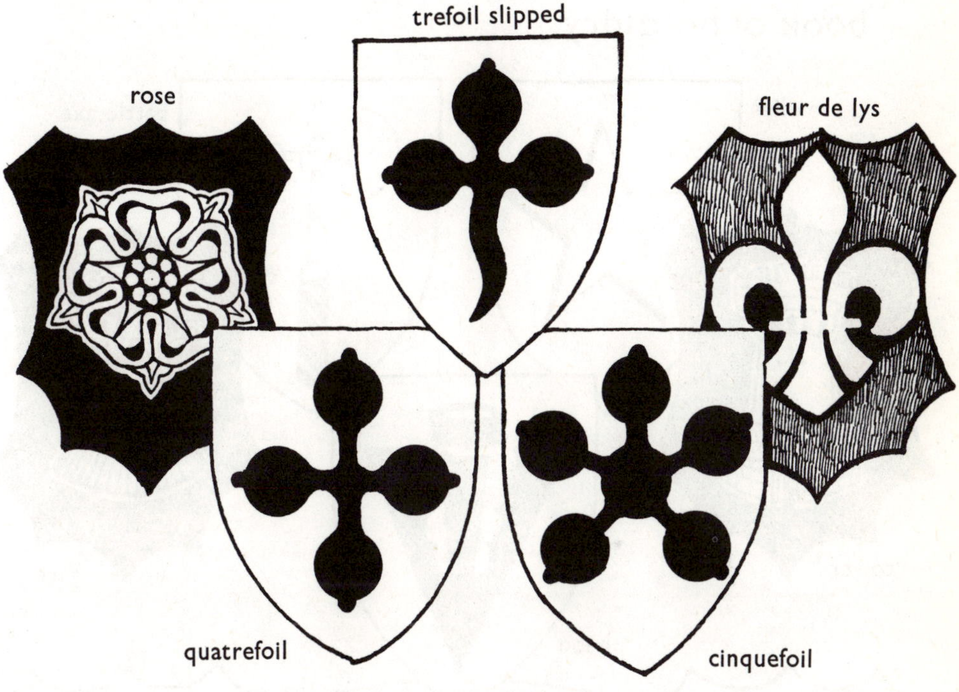

There are all sorts of other charges (things and shapes) used in coats of arms. Those in the next picture are only a few of the better-known ones. To show every object ever used as a charge in heraldry would need at least an extra hundred pages! If you keep your eyes open you will soon discover other charges. Collect them for your own scrap-book of heraldry.

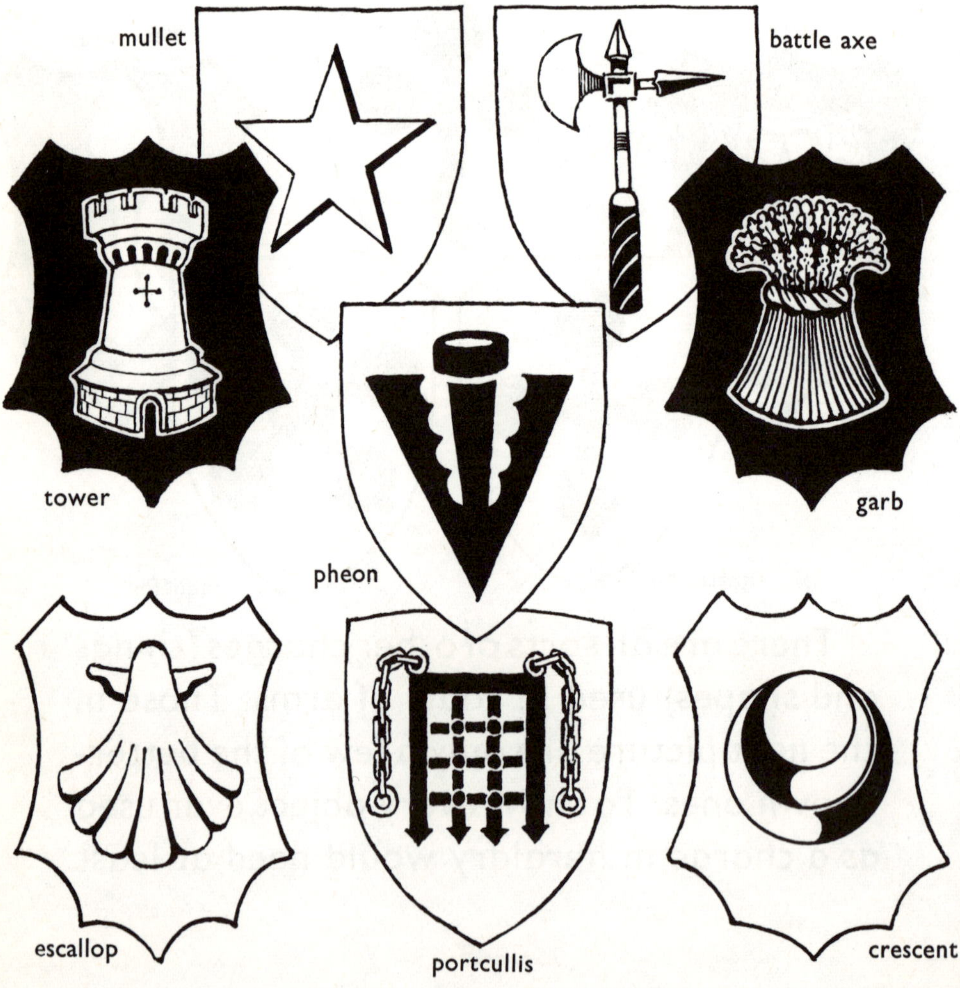

Lines and divisions

There is one other thing to learn about designing a shield. The heralds may use *lines* in various ways. Straight lines can be rather dull, so they use lines of different shapes. Here are some ordinaries drawn with various lines, together with the names given to the lines.

bend engrailed

pale indented

bend invected

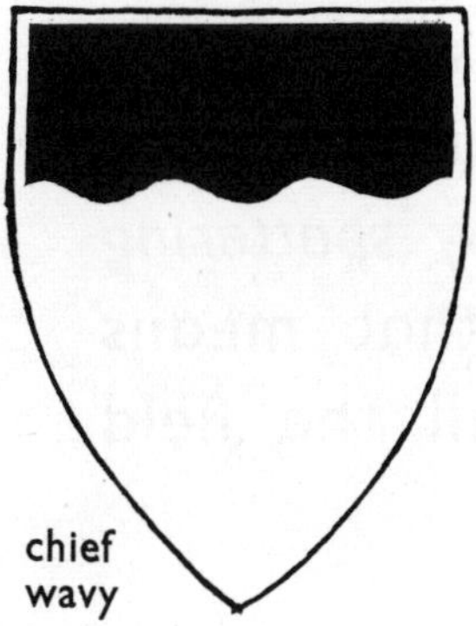

chief wavy

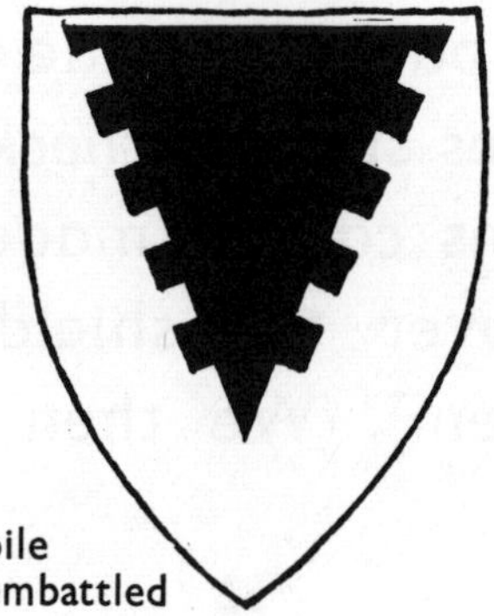

pile embattled

fess nebuly

Lines can also be used to divide up the field on a shield. It can be divided in various ways with different types of lines, as you see here.

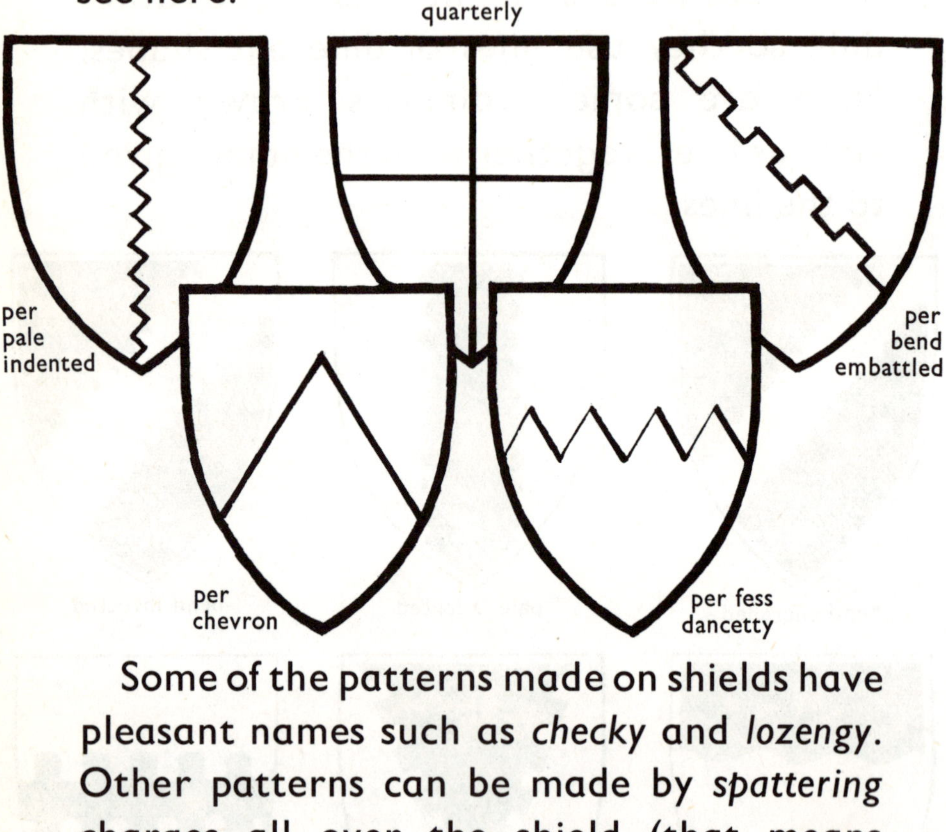

Some of the patterns made on shields have pleasant names such as *checky* and *lozengy*. Other patterns can be made by *spattering* charges all over the shield (that means scattering them). We then call the field *semy*, which is from a French word meaning "sown"–as you sow wheat, for example. Not only may the fields be divided and patterned, but so may the charges on them.

The pictures below, and in colour next to page 55, give you an idea of what can be done just by using dividing lines and patterns.

checky

lozengy

semy of roses

BLAZONING

Heralds have a special way of describing a coat of arms. It is called *blazoning*. To blazon a coat of arms is to talk or write about it in such a way that it can be drawn exactly from the description.

In blazoning arms the heralds use the special words that you have read so far in this book, and many others also. Blazon is a sort of language, and it is quite hard to learn, but can be fun. Perhaps you can find a bigger book which will teach you more about it, but here are a few rules to start you off. If you learn and understand the two rules below you will be able to blazon a lot of simple coats of arms.

1. First describe the colour of the field. If the shield is divided, start off with the word

The Queen's arms

Arms using lines and patterns

"Per", then name the kind of dividing line, such as "pale wavy". Next mention the colour in chief (the top colour) first, then the other colour. If the field is divided "per pale" (that is, in two upright parts), say the colour of the dexter part first, which is on your left as you look at it. If it is "semy" (spattered with shapes, or *charges*) mention the background colour first, then say "semy of" whatever the charges are. Then say the colour of the charges–for example, "vert semy of martlets or".

2. Now mention the name of any *ordinary* shown on the shield, then the type of lines with which it is drawn, then its colour (for example, "a fess nebuly argent"). If there is no ordinary, say instead the most important charge. If, like a lion, it can be drawn in various positions, next mention its position and lastly its colour (for example, "a boar passant gules").

Now let us practise blazoning, with the three shields shown below. Keep looking back in this book for the words to use for colours, lines, shapes, positions, and so on.

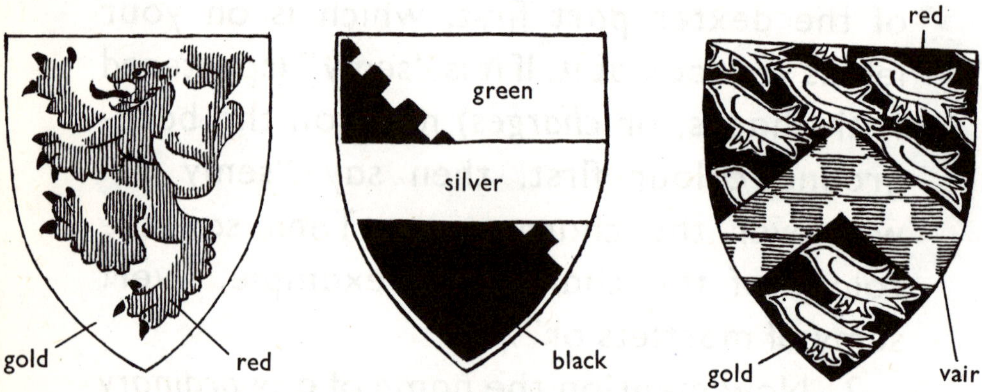

The colour of the first one is gold, so you will start with "Or". There is a lion on the field, so you will say "Or a lion". The lion's position is *rampant*, so the blazon will now read "Or a lion rampant". Lastly you must mention the lion's colour, which is red, or *gules*.

So the full blazon will read:

Or a lion rampant gules.

The next one is in two parts, so you start with "Per" and name the dividing line. This follows the direction of the ordinary called a *bend*, so you say "Per bend". The line is the one called *embattled*, so you will say "Per bend embattled".

Next you name the colours, the top one coming first. This is green (*vert*), and the bottom colour is black (*sable*). So now you have "Per bend embattled vert and sable".

Lastly you say the charge, followed by its colour. The charge here is a *fess* (look back at page 40), and it is silver (*argent*). So the full blazon will read:

Per bend embattled vert and sable a fess argent.

The third shield has a patterned field, with martlets spattered on it (*semy*). So first you say the red background colour–

"Gules". Then you say "semy of martlets", then what colour the martlets are. (They are gold–*or*). This gives you "Gules semy of martlets or".

There is an ordinary (the one called a *chevron*) on this field, so you give its name, then its colour. Do you remember this colour? It is the fur called *vair*. So your full blazon now is:

Gules, semy of martlets or, chevron vair.

It is not too difficult, is it? Now look at the arms below, and see if you can work out how the blazon was written.

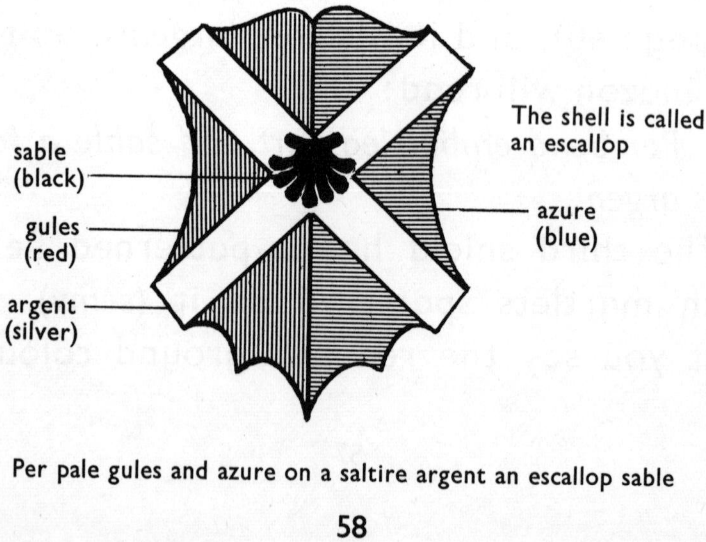

Per pale gules and azure on a saltire argent an escallop sable

INDEX

There are also some lists of special names or words, as follows:

Printed in Great Britain
at the Alden Press, Oxford
Colour Plates printed by
Compton Printing Ltd, London and Aylesbury
Bound by Kemp Hall Bindery, Oxford